What is...
HALLOWEEN

Find our books at Amazon, Barnes & Noble, Walmart, Books-A-Million, OverDrive, Kobo, Lulu, IngramSpark, and more!

Like, Share and Follow us on Facebook, Instagram, Threads, Pinterest, YouTube, LinkedIn, and more! Find our Sloths Love to Read Podcast on Spotify, Apple Podcast. Amazon Music, Pandora, and more!

www.SlothDreamsBooks.com

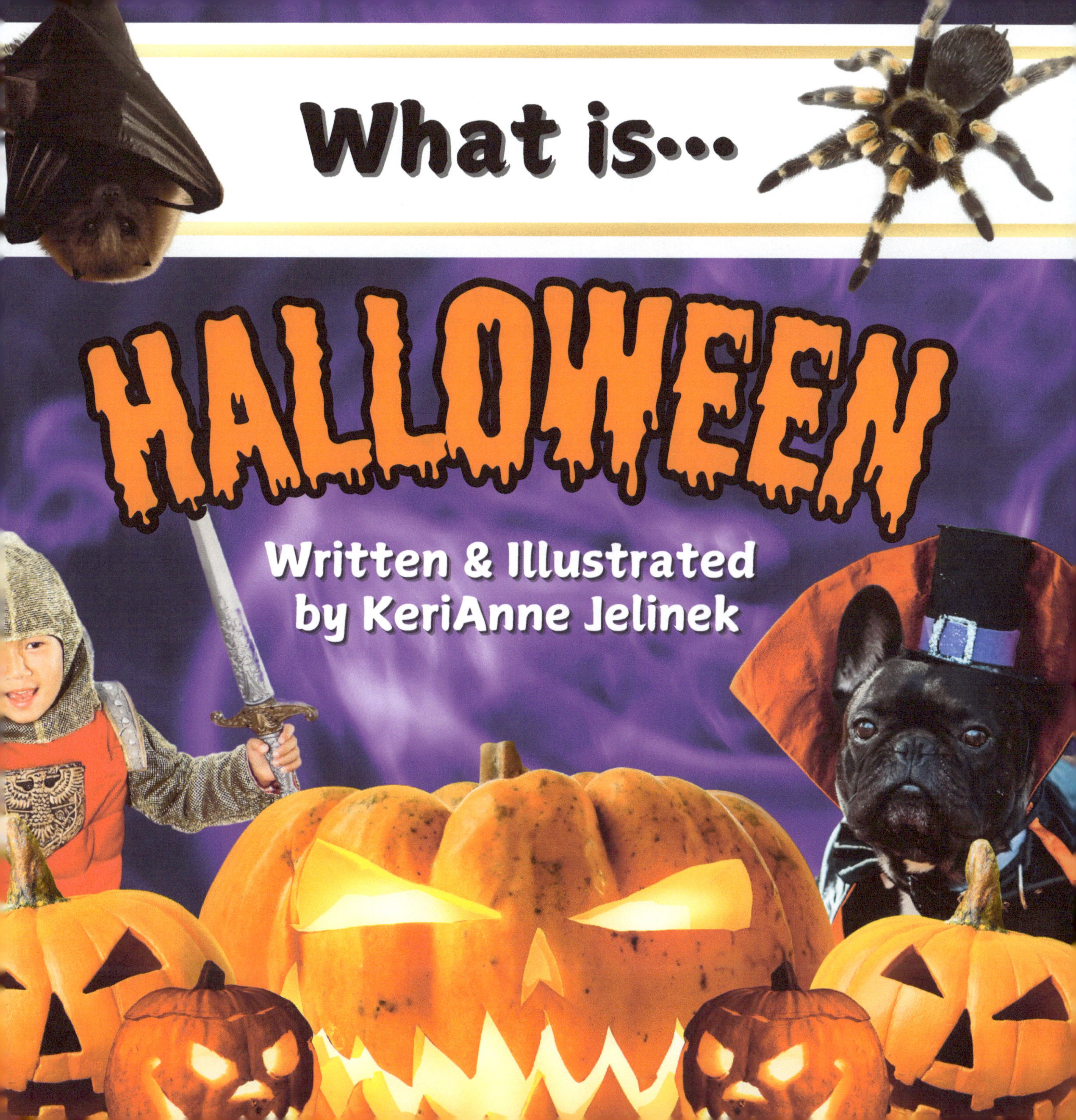

What is...
HALLOWEEN
Written & Illustrated
by KeriAnne Jelinek

What is Halloween?

Halloween is a magical holiday filled with costumes, candy, and spooky fun, but why do we celebrate it? Let's uncover the true and factual reasons behind Halloween's celebrations.

Long ago, in ancient Gaelic countries, people believed that during this special time of the year, the spirits of their ancestors would return to visit them. To welcome and honor these spirits, they celebrated the medieval festival of Samhain.

Samhain also marked the end of the harvest season when farmers gather their crops. In ancient times, people celebrated with feasts and shared their bounty with others. This tradition of giving thanks and sharing is part of Samhain's history. Eventually, Samhain, over hundreds of years, became Halloween. Samhain and Halloween both have roots in pagan and Christian traditions.

Around a thousand years ago, a special day was set aside to honor all the saints in the Christian religion as well. This day was called "All Saints' Day" and was celebrated on November 1st. Halloween, also known as "All Hallows' Eve," is the night before All Saints' Day, and it became a time for people to remember those who had passed away.

In the past, people believed that Samhain, was a time when the boundary between our world and the spirit world was thin. To protect themselves from evil spirits, they would light bonfires and wear costumes to disguise themselves.

Samhain was a time of change. It is the time when trees shed their leaves, animals prepare for winter, and people would try to predict the future. The early Gaelic people played games and told fortunes to find out what lay ahead.

As time passed, Samhain evolved into Halloween, a day of fun and celebration. People of all ages came together to dress up in costumes, go trick-or-treating, carve pumpkins, and enjoy tasty treats.

Halloween is celebrated in many countries, especially in the United States, Canada, the United Kingdom, and Ireland. People from all walks of life join in the festivities, making it a joyous and inclusive holiday for children and adults alike.

So, why do we celebrate Halloween? It's a wonderful blend of traditions from the past, honoring loved ones, celebrating the harvest, and having lots of fun. Halloween has a rich history that brings people together to enjoy this magical and spooky holiday.

Halloween
Dress-Up:
You can dress up in a
creative costume,
like a spooky ghost or
a heroic superhero.

Trick-or-
Treat:
You can go
trick-or-
treating in your
neighborhood,
collecting
delicious candies
or other yummy
treats.

Costume
Parade:
You can have
a costume
parade with
your friends
and show off
your
fantastic
Halloween
costumes.

Pumpkin Carving:
You can carve a pumpkin and create your very own jack-o'-lantern.

Party Games:
You can bob for apples
in a big, fun-filled tub
or bucket of water.

Movie Fun:
You can have a movie night with your favorite Halloween-themed movies or cartoons.

Creepy Crafts:
You can make creepy-
crawly crafts, like
paper spiders and bats.

Halloween Hunt:
You can go on a spooky scavenger hunt, searching for hidden treasures.

Cozy Campfire:
You can gather around a campfire and tell eerie or spooky ghost stories.

DANGER
HAUNTED
HOUSE
Spooky Fun:
You can visit a haunted house
or an amusement park for a
thrilling adventure.

Party Time:

You can host a costume party with your friends and family, that feature games, music, and dancing.

Halloween Bowling:
You can go bowling with your friends and family, while wearing your Halloween costume for a spooky and fun game.

Snack
Zombie-
Attack:
You can
create
monster-
themed
snacks, like
"mummy dogs"
or "witches'
brew."

Face Painting:
You can have your face painted with cute, scary or funny design.

Pumpkin Painting:
You can paint and decorate pumpkins with colorful patterns and faces.

HAPPY
HALLOWEEN

9 783606 814332